Revised Edition

Alex Rodriguez

By Jeffrey Zuehlke

AMAZING ATHLETES

Lerner Publications Company/Minneapolis

Lerner Publications Company
A division of Lerner Publishing Group, Inc.
241 First Avenue North
Minneapolis, MN 55401 U.S.A.

Website address: www.lernerbooks.com

Library of Congress Cataloging-in-Publication Data

Zuehlke, Jeffrey, 1968-
    Alex Rodriguez / by Jeffrey Zuehlke. — Rev. ed.
        p.   cm. — (Amazing athletes)
    Includes bibliographical references and index.
    ISBN 978-0-8225-8871-9 (lib. bdg. : alk. paper)
    1. Rodriguez, Alex, 1975– —Juvenile literature. 2. Baseball players—United States—Biography—Juvenile literature. I. Title.
    GV865.R62Z84 2009
    796.357'092—dc22 [B]   2008028269

Manufactured in the United States of America
1 2 3 4 5 6 — BP — 14 13 12 11 10 09

TABLE OF CONTENTS

500-Home Run Club   4

Growing Up   10

Amazing Athlete   14

Superstar   18

One of the Best   23

Selected Career Highlights   29

Glossary   30

Further Reading & Websites   31

Index   32

Many people come out to watch the Yankees play every game.

500-Home Run Club

Alex Rodriguez stared out at the pitcher. The star third baseman spun the bat in his hands and waited for the ball as the crowd roared around him.

Alex and the New York Yankees were playing against the Kansas City Royals. The game was held at Yankee Stadium in New York, and the hometown fans were hoping to see history made. Alex had 499 **home runs**. Only 21 players in the history of **Major League Baseball (MLB)** had ever hit 500 or more home runs. Would Alex become the 22nd player to reach this mark?

The Yankees' third baseman was feeling a lot of pressure. He hit his 499th home run one week earlier. He came to bat 27 times since then but failed to hit another home run. He wanted to hit number 500 in front of the fans at Yankee Stadium.

The Yankees played at Yankee Stadium from 1923 to 2008.

Royals pitcher Kyle Davies threw a **sinker** toward home plate. He was hoping that Alex would swing at the low ball. With a runner on first base, Davies wanted the Yankees' slugger to hit into a **double play**. But the ball didn't sink as much as Davies had hoped. "The ball came back over the middle a little bit," he said after the game.

Alex swings at Royals pitcher Kyle Davies's pitch.

Alex took a vicious swing and made contact. The ball sailed through the air toward the seats in left field. As the crowd jumped to its feet, the ball soared over the outfield wall for a home run. Alex raised both arms in the air as he ran toward first base. He had made history with his 500th home run!

Alex rounds the bases after hitting his 500th home run.

Alex's teammates Derek Jeter *(right)* and Bobby Abreu *(center)* congratulate him as he reaches home plate.

The crowd went crazy as Alex rounded the bases. He was greeted at home plate with high fives and hugs from teammates Derek Jeter and Bobby Abreu. All of Alex's teammates came out of the **dugout** to pat him on the back. Everyone was excited for the newest member of the 500-home run club.

Alex's amazing feat made history in more ways than one. He was just 32 years and eight days old, making him the youngest player in the history of MLB to hit 500 home runs. He was just the third player to hit his 500th home run as a member of the Yankees, joining Babe Ruth and Mickey Mantle. Ruth and Mantle are two of the greatest baseball players of all time.

Alex was finally able to relax after the game. He was relieved to have his 500th home run out of the way. He was glad that he hit it at Yankee Stadium. "To do it at home and to wear this beautiful uniform that I appreciate and respect so much, it's special," Alex said. "New York is a special place."

Alex smiles while talking to reporters after the game.

Alex was born in New York City. His family lived in the Washington Heights area, which includes Fort Tryon Park.

GROWING UP

Alex Rodriguez was born in New York City on July 27, 1975. He was the youngest of three children. Alex's father, Victor Rodriguez, had played professional baseball. Victor taught Alex how to swing a bat and how to catch and throw the ball. Soon Alex and his friends were playing baseball every day.

When Alex was eight years old, his family moved to Kendall, Florida, near Miami. Alex played baseball whenever he could. He practiced hitting, fielding, and baserunning. He dreamed of being a Major League Baseball (MLB) player. He hoped to play in the **World Series** one day.

Alex grew quickly. Soon he was taller, stronger, and faster than most kids his age. Alex often played with athletes a few years older than he was. Playing with bigger kids was a challenge. It made Alex a better player.

Victor Rodriguez was born in the Dominican Republic, a country in the Caribbean Sea. Baseball is very popular there.

Life was going great for Alex until just after his ninth birthday. At that time, his father left the family. Victor Rodriguez moved away and never came back.

Alex was heartbroken. But playing baseball helped him feel better.

As a kid, Alex spent a lot of time playing sports at the Boys & Girls Club near his home in Florida. As an adult, Alex still spends a lot of time at the Boys & Girls Club. He has given lots of his time and money to help support the organization.

Alex was a good student in spite of family problems.

Alex played shortstop for Westminster Christian School in Miami. The small high school had one of the best high school baseball teams in the country.

Meanwhile, Alex's mother, Lourdes, worked hard to take care of Alex, his sister, Susy, and his brother, Joe.

Lourdes encouraged Alex to keep playing baseball and to practice hard. She also made sure that Alex worked in school. Alex loved learning. He studied and earned good grades.

Lourdes told Alex not to brag about his baseball talents. She taught Alex to be polite and treat people with respect.

Alex graduated from Westminster in 1993. The school named him to its baseball Hall of Fame.

AMAZING ATHLETE

As a teenager, Alex was one of the best high school baseball players in the United States. **Scouts** from MLB teams came to watch him play. Scouts liked the way he practiced hard, studied hard, and treated people with respect.

At first, Alex was unhappy that the Seattle Mariners had drafted him. The Mariners had been a losing team for many years. But he soon became excited about playing with Mariner superstars Ken Griffey Jr., Edgar Martinez, Randy Johnson, and Jay Buhner.

In June 1993, the Seattle Mariners picked Alex first in the MLB **draft.** Alex's dream of being a major league ballplayer was close to coming true. But he would have to work hard to earn a spot on the team.

Alex started the 1994 season in the **minor leagues.** He quickly showed how good he was and how fast he was learning. He hit the ball hard and made big plays in the field. By the middle of the season, the Mariners wanted Alex to play for the big league club.

Alex played his first major league game on July 7, 1994. He was just 18 years old. Alex played for the Mariners for 26 days. Sometimes he played great. Other times he made mistakes. Alex still had a lot to learn. The Mariners sent him back to the minor leagues to get better.

Alex is only the third 18-year-old since 1900 to play shortstop in the major leagues.

In 1995, Alex bounced up and down between the minor leagues and the Mariners. He became unhappy at times. Alex wanted to stay with the Mariners, but he was still young and needed to improve. At the end of the season, he promised to work extra hard to become the Mariners starting shortstop the next season.

Alex worked hard to stay on the Mariners. But after being sent down to the minor leagues three times, he almost quit.

Alex improved his batting and fielding skills in 1996.

SUPERSTAR

That winter, Alex exercised and practiced six days a week. In 1996, he arrived at **spring training** in top shape.

Alex's hard work paid off. He quickly became one of the league's toughest hitters, with a .358 **batting average.** He slugged 36 home runs and 54 **doubles**. He scored 141 runs and collected 123 **runs batted in (RBI).** Alex made dozens of great plays in the field too.

Alex was selected to his first American League All-Star Team. His teammates and fans gave him a nickname, A-Rod. Alex became one of the most popular players in baseball.

Alex had another super year in 1997. In fact, the whole Mariner team did well. They won their division, earning a spot in the playoffs. But the Mariners lost to the Baltimore Orioles in the **division** series. Alex was disappointed but planned to practice hard and have another great season.

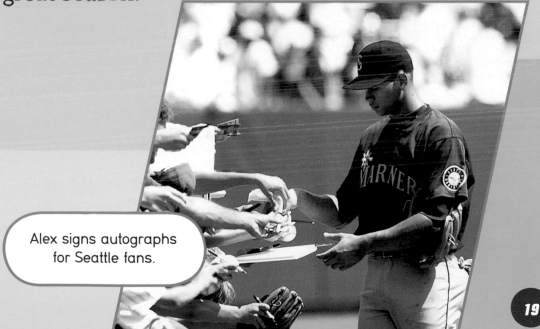

Alex signs autographs for Seattle fans.

The only "40–40" men in major league history are Alex, Barry Bonds, and Jose Canseco.

In 1998, Alex became only the third "40–40" player in major league history. He hit 42 home runs and stole 46 bases. The next season, he became the first shortstop to hit more than 40 home runs two years in a row.

In 2000, Alex made it three years in a row, hitting 41 home runs. He also led the Mariners to the playoffs again. They beat the Chicago White Sox in the division series, but they lost to the New York Yankees in the **American League Champion Series (ALCS)**.

By this time, many people were calling Alex the best player in baseball. Some were saying he might be the best baseball player *ever*.

Alex tries not to let all of the praise go to his head. He knows he has talent. But he also knows he has to work hard to be the best. "He's a down to earth guy," said one of his teammates. "He works [hard] just like everybody else."

Baseball experts call Alex a "five-tool player." That means he's great at the five most important baseball skills. He can run fast, catch the ball well, throw well, hit for a high batting average, and hit for power.

As he became more famous, Alex stayed focused on his game.

Alex liked his Mariner teammates. But he was ready for a change.

After the 2000 season, Alex became a **free agent.** He could choose to play with any team that wanted him. The Mariners, New York Mets, Texas Rangers, and several other teams wanted Alex to play for them.

Alex chose the Texas Rangers. He signed a contract to play for the Rangers for 10 years. In return, the team agreed to pay Alex $252 million over 10 years. It was the richest contract in sports history!

Alex throws to first base during his first season with the Texas Rangers.

ONE OF THE BEST

Alex had three super seasons with the Rangers. In 2001, he led the American League in home runs with 52. He played in every game and made many great plays as shortstop. In 2002, Alex smacked 57 home runs—tops in the league again.

Alex worked hard for the Rangers. But he wanted to play in the World Series.

The next season, Alex led the American League in home runs for the third year in a row, hitting 47. At the end of the 2003 season, Alex was voted the American League's Most Valuable Player (MVP).

But even though Alex played well, the Rangers struggled. The team finished in last place in 2003. Alex loved the Texas fans and his Ranger teammates, but he wanted to play on a winning team.

Before the 2004 season, the New York Yankees offered to trade for Alex. But there was one problem. The Yankees already had a great shortstop, Derek Jeter. Would Alex change positions to play for the Yankees?

Alex quickly agreed to the switch. He became the new third baseman for the Yankees.

"I can't express . . . how grateful I am to be a Yankee," Alex wrote. "I just don't have words for it."

Derek Jeter (left), Alex, and Jason Giambi joke while doing exercises at spring training in 2004. The Yankees train at Legends Field in Tampa, Florida.

With Alex leading the way, the Yankees had a super season. They won 101 games to finish in first place in their division. Alex hit 36 home runs and knocked in 106 RBI.

The Yankees made it to the 2004 ALCS against the Boston Red Sox. The Yankees had three thrilling victories. But the Red Sox won

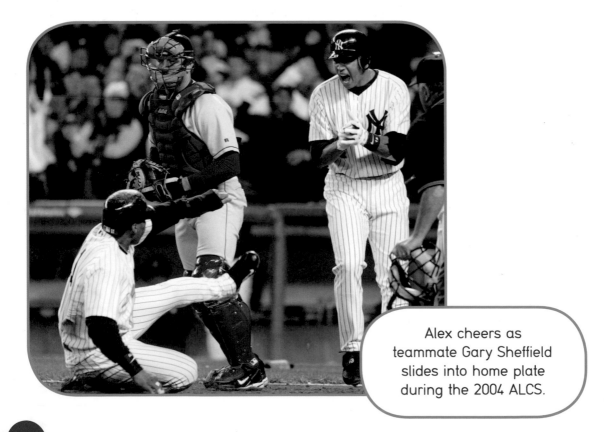

Alex cheers as teammate Gary Sheffield slides into home plate during the 2004 ALCS.

the next four games. Alex's team didn't make it to the World Series. But they knew they would keep trying.

Alex has kept up his amazing play in New York. In 2005, he led the American League in home runs with 48. He

Alex bats during the 2006 All-Star Game in Pittsburgh, Pennsylvania.

was also named American League MVP for the second time. He was elected to the American League All-Star Team again in 2006. In 2007, he led the American League in home runs with 54. And he was named American League Most Valuable Player for the third time!

Actor Mark Wahlberg, Alex, and Ken Griffey Jr. *(back row left to right)* meet with members of the Boys & Girls Clubs of America.

Alex knows he's lucky to be so rich and successful. He tries to help others as often as he can. He works with the Boys & Girls Clubs in Miami, Dallas, and New York City. He has given money to help build ballparks and gyms for kids. Alex also visits schools. He tells students to work hard to achieve their dreams.

Alex's dream is to win the World Series. He'll keep working hard for the Yankees to make that dream come true.

Selected Career Highlights

2008 finished third in the American League in home runs (35)

2007 voted the American League's MVP
led the American League in home runs (54)
became the youngest player ever to reach 500 home runs (32 years, 8 days)

2006 selected to his tenth American League All-Star Team

2005 voted the American League's MVP
led the American League in home runs (48)

2004 selected to his ninth American League All-Star Team

2003 voted the American League's MVP
became the youngest player ever to reach 300 home runs (27 years, 8 months)
selected to his eighth American League All-Star Team
led the American League in home runs (47) for the third straight year

2002 led the major leagues in home runs (57), RBI (142), and total bases (389)
selected to his seventh American League All-Star Team

2001 led the American League in home runs (52), runs scored (133), and total bases (393)
selected to his sixth American League All-Star Team

2000 selected to his fifth American League All-Star Team

1999 selected to his fourth American League All-Star Team

1998 became the third "40–40" player in MLB history, hitting 42 home runs and stealing 46 bases
selected to his third American League All-Star Team

1997 selected to his second American League All-Star Team

1996 selected to his first American League All-Star Team

Glossary

American League Championship Series (ALCS): a seven-game series played by the winners of the two American League Division Series. The team that wins four games in the series goes on to the World Series.

batting average: a number that describes how often a player makes a base hit. Major League Baseball's best batters usually hit above .300.

division: a group of teams within a league. Major League Baseball's 30 teams are divided into six divisions. In the first round of championship playoffs, teams play a five-game Division Series.

double play: a play in which two outs are made

doubles: hits that allow the batter to reach second base safely

draft: a yearly event in which professional teams in a sport are given the chance to choose new players from a selected group

dugout: the area next to the field where a baseball team sits

free agent: a player whose contract with one team has ended, freeing him to join any team that offers to sign him

home runs: hits that allow the batter to circle all the bases to score a run

Major League Baseball (MLB): the top group of professional baseball teams in North America, divided into the National League and the American League

minor leagues: leagues ranked below the major league

runs batted in (RBI): the number of runners able to score on a batter's hit, including the batter

scouts: people who watch and judge athletes' skills

sinker: a pitch that sinks when it gets near home plate

spring training: a period from February through March when baseball teams train for the upcoming season

World Series: MLB's championship, played each season between the best American League team and the best National League team

Further Reading & Websites

Donovan, Sandy. *Derek Jeter*. Minneapolis: Lerner Publications Company, 2004.

Patrick, Jean L. S. *The Girl Who Struck Out Babe Ruth*. Minneapolis: Millbrook Press, 2000.

Thomas, Keltie. *How Baseball Works*. Toronto: Maple Tree Press, 2008.

Stewart, Mark. *Long Ball: The Legend and Lore of the Home Run*. Minneapolis: Millbrook Press, 2006.

AROD.com
http://arod.mlb.com/players/rodriguez_alex/index.jsp
The official site of Alex Rodriguez includes A-Rod news, stats, and photographs.

Boys & Girls Club of America
http://www.bgca.org
Visit this site to learn more about Alex's favorite organization, the Boys & Girls Club of America.

Espn.com
http://espn.com
Espn.com covers all the major professional sports, including Major League Baseball.

Major League Baseball
http://www.mlb.com
The official site of Major League Baseball provides up-to-date news and statistics of all 30 Major League teams and every major league player.

Sports Illustrated Kids
http://www.sikids.com
The *Sports Illustrated Kids* website covers all sports, including baseball.

Index

Abreu, Bobby, 8
Boston Red Sox, 26–27
Boys & Girls Clubs, 28

Davies, Kyle, 6

Jeter, Derek, 8, 25

Kansas City Royals, 4, 6

Mantle, Mickey, 9

New York Yankees, 4–9, 20, 25–27

Rodriguez, Alex: as an All-Star,
    19, 27; batting, 4–7, 10, 11, 18,
    20; childhood, 10–13; fielding,
    11, 15, 18, 23; as a "five-tool
    player," 21; as a "40–40" player,
    20; in high school, 14; in minor
leagues, 15, 16–17; as a New
    York Yankee, 4–9, 25–27; as a
    Seattle Mariner, 14–17, 18–21; as
    a Texas Ranger, 22, 23–24
Rodriguez, Joe (brother), 13
Rodriguez, Lourdes (mother), 13
Rodriguez, Susy (sister), 13
Rodriguez, Victor (father), 10, 12

Ruth, Babe, 9

2000 American League
    Championship Series (ALCS), 20
2004 American League
    Championship Series (ALCS),
    26–27

World Series, 11, 27, 28

Yankee Stadium, 4–5, 9

Photo Acknowledgments

The images in this book are used with the permission of: © Rob Tringali/
SportsChrome/Getty Images, p. 4; © Jim McIsaac/Getty Images, p. 5;
AP Photo/Bill Kostroun, pp. 6, 29; AP Photo/Frank Franklin II, pp. 7, 8, 9;
© Tony Linck/SuperStock, p. 10; © Tom Bean/CORBIS, p. 11; Seth Poppel
Yearbook Library, pp. 12, 14; © David Bergman/CORBIS, p. 13; © Rob Tringali/
SportsChrome, pp. 16, 22, 24; © Michael Zito/SportsChrome, p. 17; © Jeff
Carlick/SportsChrome, pp. 18, 21; © John Klein/SportsChrome, p. 19; AP
Photo/Tony Dejak, p. 23; REUTERS/Peter Muhly, p. 25; REUTERS/Shannon
Stapleton, p. 26; © Jamie Squire/Getty Images, p. 27; © Nancy Kaszermann/
ZUMA Press, p. 28.

Front Cover: © Rob Tringali/SportsChrome.